Totalité Conformité Anxiété

By
Brian Matta

Black Centipede Press

Black Centipede Press
Denver, CO
blackcentipedepress@gmail.com

ISBN #: 978-1-7353275-0-1

Design, layout, and edits: Brian Matta

Cover Art: Brian Matta

Acknowledgement:

“Attempting Thursday,” published in Issue #6 *Newtown Literary*
“A Parallax View,” published in Issue #199 *No, Dear Magazine*
“Straphanger,” and “Sequestered,” published in Brine Literary Issue #2

Totalité

Conformité

32. Dear Applicant for Arrest
33. Dear Applicant for Arrest
35. Dear Applicant for Arrest
36. Dear Applicant for Arrest
37. Dear Applicant for Arrest
38. Dear Applicant for Arrest
39. Dear Applicant for Arrest
40. Dear Applicant for Arrest
41. Dear Applicant for Arrest
42. Dear Applicant for Arrest

Anxiété

43.that man made
44. down the road
45. on the job
46. what the but
47. here to help
48. everything but nickels
49. but what was
50. can't you see
51. the next war
52. used to be
53. trouble with doors
54. as if still
55. it's not that
56. not a member
57. an implied stop
58. I'm so sorry
59. a bus stop
60. if you want
61. all the lines

Totalité

Yesterday

America fell into the sea
and no one could get to work
because of the traffic jam
caused by the land bridge
between Canada and Mexico
being out we all abandoned
our cars to check out the
latest beaches but found
piles of bodies laying
on the damp sand
hogging all the sun

Poverty

but the TV won't work
no matter how much
we pretend it does
and hope smears itself
along the windows
becoming a hard and
ugly thing as morning
erodes into day the only
progress is our bodies
becoming blackening
shapes of mildew
waiting to see
if the night decides
to show

Straphanger

Forced light shines on
the sagging rails as
the train pulls
into the station
where pedestrians
no longer jump
over Tuesday's turnstile
into Wednesday's abyss
but stand in line
patiently to pay the fair
for Thursday
where a better barbarism
awaits

Bitter Bureaucracies

where
there
here no
here
there no
there
here
no there
here
there
no

Attempting Thursday

Feeling unappreciated by the lawnmower
the long uncut grass tries to cover up
two broken air conditioners in a bald
patch of mud facing each other
as if having a casual conversation
about the end of things and
the dandelions are attempting
Thursday still hiding behind
the abandon shack trying
to avoid Wednesday
and an appointment
with the lawnmower
the dull guillotine

Modern Ruins

store fronts joining each other
are still bodies in motion
silhouetted against the neon sky
where patrons sit drinking
notions of coffee and
quotients of cheese
trying not to articulate
the horror of these stucco
monoliths liberating
the landscape from
the placid plainness
of prairie grass but
the wind shifts
as if a conclusion
had been reached
and the stores
lay empty as
corn husks
hardened and yellowing
wanting to be
blown away

Antebellum

that window is open and closing
quick as smoke rises from
the tree line but
Can I ask you a question
yes but make it quick
where does the barbed wire go
not here but further
down the road

Epilogue

after the war
we thought we'd be
dust but instead
we wait around
for the end trying
to escape from
the effigy
that is everyday

Pedestrian

cars slide along
the obsidian blacktop
with no particular place to go
dodging pedestrians
in the decaying day
turning them into
burnt matches
their shadows staining
the concrete landscape with
remnants of an idiot Iowa
the rusting crops and old barren
trucks long out of use
elongating and twisting
in the fatigue of day
where the figures wait for
the long knife of night
to sever its ties and have
peace until the next dawn

Winter's Firing Squad

we met in the mass grave of summer
when love was a slow burning lye
calmly stinging our skin
we were militants then
dead but soon resurrected
only to die better tomorrow
now we are descending
staircases asleep on the porch
sounding the alarm on those
who approach the door

Empty Faces

We do not burn like cities
Or stale light bulbs
But as compulsion
Maneuvering cautiously around the room
Meeting but never touching each other
Emptying out on the floor
With the routine of handshakes
Until we identify completely
With the mere posturing of ourselves

All-or-None Law

fatigue
of this phenomenon
will act as an
obstacle exciting
an impulse which
travels through
protoplasm
evidence of an
actual liberation
the development
of a minute

Can’t Get Away

Don’t talk to me about this or that America
Nationality is just the perversion
you’re trapped in
like old furniture
being reupholstered
we have a new style
with the same anxiety
of right angles
in someone else’s house
but I could never pay attention
to the background of things
like a bent coat rack longing
to be a used car
that can drive hundreds of miles
without refilling
but what you mean by escape

Sequestered

The sun drags itself
back and forth
along the blue horizon
pacing in a daze since
the people voted to
suspend the night
indefinitely deciding sleep
was inefficient
the world shrivels at its cornices
and everything begins to have
a brown patina like a vulgarity
that wouldn’t be washed away
and the flowers bend back
a collective plea
for the veneer of night

A Parallax View

These bitter estates
grow like crooked teeth
out of long uncut grass
and stand as an example
that man is forgetful
or perhaps neglect
is a suitable revenge
like a diluted Michigan
with its windows
all boarded up
longing for a bureaucratic life
causal and leaderless
the letter is not lost
only pending
still waiting while
stagnate water collects
but there is a black line being
drawn along the horizon
where new landmasses form
you wish to place yourself there
but there is no place for you

A Prelude to Hope

the operator died
leaving an aperture as its substitute
where everything flowed from
giving sustenance
like an old rag
not a fruitful tree
until it too
corroded away admitting
an endless transmission
illuminating from the
impossible torpor of night
like freedom
misery’s loneliness hue

Empty Sketch

emerging from
a gravity of silence
empty and incomplete
to do one last thing
before returning
to the void
revenge and anger
no longer exist
now only the sword
a beacon
consuming
the night

La Jetee

The season's apparatus is obsolete
a neutered spring piled on
the yellowing winter
rotting not yet permitted
to die and dignity peels
like paint from the corridors
of trees where a new consensus
is reached that the door
once opened has now closed

Waiting

Nervous about the future
whether it will be
a lack of chairs
or piles of clothes
with the bodies cut out
but worrying no more
when we become
planks of wood
to prop up cornices
and windows for
a new world and
feel better we
don’t remember
what we used to be

Apocalypse

and in the distance
a car horn blaring
seeming to go on
forever like poverty
boring without end

Conformité

Dear Applicant for Arrest

Thank you for your interest
But we are going with another applicant
Whose deeds are more important
They built a bomb
And tried to become a god
This application shows you're depressed
And the Arresting Committee is not impressed
Most men at your economic level beat their family
You're a statistic not a threat to society
Please stop wasting our time
Until you come back with better crimes
Help us do our job
Signed the disinterested mob

Dear Applicant for Arrest

Please visit the arresting station
To create a new application
In order to become a citizen it must be attested
Under Applicant Enrollment 004.02 you will be arrested
After you have been thoroughly brutalized
Your application can finally be authorized
And you will be put into our system
Given full liberty and freedom
Eligible to register for a home and a car
Walk down the street and go into a bar
If you do not comply
We will have to say good-bye
Your application will be dismissed
This is your final notice
You have 15 days to fill out the form
Please come down and conform

Dear Applicant for Arrest

You were not in attendance
At yesterday's spring dance
And you missed the human sacrifice at the library
which was a community event and mandatory
And we have complaints about last week's orgy
Stating you were standing around acting ordinary
Which is against the self-expression clause
All citizens must expression themselves at times without pause
And considering your most recent absents
We have decided on punishments
And created a schedule to receive them all
Everyday from 9 to 5 spring to fall
Including sleep deprivation, starvation, et cetera
And if there is time perhaps some minor abuse as extra
Until you see the errors of your ways
And recognize community participation is everyday
You must learn that it is a full-time job
Sincerely the Punctuality Committee for the Community's Mob

Dear Applicant for Arrest

This notice is to congratulate you on ignoring what we said
All doors in neighborhoods 35-45 must be painted red
But your house's door is painted bright green
Against ordinance 55 which makes the neighborhood not obscene
Bright coloration ruins the neighborhood's veneer
That of being quaint and sincere
People no longer drive down the street
Leading to a rise in suicides that is no longer discrete
The damage you have caused is unknown
But recent reports have shown
That house ownership in the neighborhoods 35 to 37 has dropped
And the figured today have the falling rates have stopped
Emergency action has to be taken
Please report to the arresting station
Thank you
The Council of Housing and Dismantling You

Dear Applicant for Arrest

We were looking over your application for arrest
What we saw from surveillance and criminality tests
Was discrepancies in your allegations
Please go down to your local office and review your application
There are many examples
Of your criminal acts here are a few sample
You stated you regularly visited the forbidden zone
We tracked your daily movements on your phone
And you were nowhere near that sector
Even with this lie it changes your arrest criteria
Under Falsified Documents Protocol 3305.02
We will not arrest you
But will plead your case in front of the Politeness Board
Once you are finished you will be erased from public record
And you be considered missing not pronounced dead
Your house will be replaced with a supermarket with freshly sliced bread
Sincerely
The Committee Disappearing You Politely

Dear Applicant for Arrest

Thank you for your submission
We were impressed by your sedition
But unfortunately we have to pass
These crimes are of your class
You need to score a 70 or better
On the rage scale to receive an acceptance letter
Your crimes appear to be boring and apathetic
Which the Arresting Council thinks is pathetic
Not clever but classified as two bit
You need to study and resubmit
An application worthy to arrest
We only want the best
In our jails
Not the petty or the frail
So hope to see you soon
Sincerely your pending doom

Dear Applicant for Arrest

We appreciate your upstanding citizenship
You always dress sharp and leave a large tip
Help the elderly across the street
Remain calm at every challenge you meet
Smile politely never bitter
That is why we're sending you this letter
If you did not hear
We may missed our quota this year
We are desperate
To fill it
So we have decided to arrest you
To continue doing what we do
We don't make the decision lightly
Knowing you work nightly
We've already told your boss
About the sacrifice you're making and the loss
To keep law and order
Not to let all we've built slip into disorder
We thank you for your contribution to society
Sincerely Your Loving Community

Dear Applicant for Arrest

We came to your apartment
For your 8 o'clock arresting appointment
But you were not there so we left you this letter
Please select a time that works better
It is a waste of resources for all the men we are sending
Just to arrest you and to have your claim still pending
An open application is something we can't afford
You could make our average wait good up and ruin our record
Which means we will lose funding
Your irresponsibility to your community is stunning
So we have made your application specialized
And you will be neutralized
Please sign and attest
A time and place for your arrest
Sincerely
The Committee of Responsibility

Dear Applicant for Arrest

We have accepted your application
About your refusing to adhere to the new language restrictions
Mainly misgendering and obscenity
Under Restriction 006.203
For example when you got your coffee
Misgendering the waitress saying he instead of calling her she
And you continue to use fuck and shit
Instead of the correct terms duck and chezit
The law states these events are offensive
And we have taken the defensive
We voted and concluded
You will be excluded
From social programs and society in general
Until you realize how rules are essential
Sincerely
Your Hurting Community

Dear Applicant for Arrest

We have heard from our informants
That you were speaking out against the government
Without the proper permit
This is your second warning so an arrest seems fit
Although under the new guidelines of reeducation
We have left some barbaric practices behind to promote civilization
Cutting the programs for the electric shock and beatings
Wanting a curriculum had more cultural meaning
Selected enhanced torture techniques
That will make your experience unique
Including pulling out finger nails
And attempting not to drown you while your head is dunk in a pale
There is so much more
We have in store
We will see you soon
Your pick up is at noon
Signed
The Committee for the Cultured and Benign

Dear Applicant for Arrest

You are receiving this notice because you did not show up for the required training class
The New Citizen Introduction and Assignment of Caste
Which is against the Law of Finding a Job
You will now be placed under the classification of Slob
Without hope or skills
Living in society unfulfilled
You will now have to a training station
Because we believe in your education
It is important for our civilization's infrastructure
And our citizens need structure
Even if you do not take it seriously
Sincerely the Welcoming Committee

Dear Applicant for Arrest

The Department of Social Ethics has been learning
About your social habits and it is concerning
We have heard that you shake people's hands for too long
Against the regulated 5 seconds which makes you come on too strong
And you make the community uncomfortable
When you blow your nose at the table
Your fellow citizens want to tell you it is not right
But they are too polite
So we are coming to arrest you
And training you what to do and not to do
Follow protocols and rubrics
On how to act in public
Until you are ready
To rejoin your community
Sincerely
The Socially Ethical and Responsibility Committee

Dear Applicant for Arrest

We hope you are becoming accommodated
To your job being automated
Please make sure to take your anti-depressant medication
To keep your negative thoughts in sedation
But we are writing you this letter
We have founded a recommendation from your former employer
And it fulfills the Reemployment Section 006.231
Stating to be reemployed the applicant has to have retesting done
So we have scheduled your arrest
For noon to retake your employment tests
To see if you should be reemployed
Or perhaps that option you should avoid
Either way you will be in our custody
And the tests will decide whether to be imprisoned or set free
Good luck and await instructions
The Department of Hiring and Implementation

Dear Applicant for Arrest

We are writing you this letter
Because we were informed by your employer
You wanted to renew your contract
But under the Recontracting Act
An employee can only stay one full year with a company
Then be set free
To maintain their status of Individuality
To move from employment to employment freely
This offense carries with it a minimum of 2 years in prison
After this sentence hopefully you will be able to have satisfaction
Be free to make choices again
And able to make short term friends
Sincerely
The Freedom Committee

Dear Applicant for Arrest

This is your final notice
Your employer told us about your absence
Your contract says you will receive
Thirty days of personal leave and thirty days of sick leave
However you have already used all your personal and sick days
And it is only May
Since you have no more leave to request
We are placing you under arrest
Whether you are sick or not
To give you proper medication and shots
So you can go back to work
And see employer as a perk
Instead of seeing it as something you need to do
We will come by and arrest you at two
See you then
The Committee Who is Wondering Where You've Been

Dear Applicant for Arrest

You are receiving this letter because it has been brought to our attention
That you have gone missing without our permission
According to reports you were last seen walking down the road
Now we have announced an emergency search mode
You have 15 days to announce your whereabouts
Or we will send an emergency arresting party out
Sincerely
The Search Committee

Dear Applicant for Arrest

We are writing you because there are reports
Of your misconduct that witnesses can support
At the public orgy you wouldn't get nude
And everyone considered that rude
There are also reports your language wasn't sexual or laud
You stood in the corner with a standoff attitude
Which the orgy committee did not appreciate
People must participate
At such events to help people let out steam
Show everyone is on the same team
This transgression
Is against our idea of progression
Corrective measures must be taken
Sincerely The Bureau of Orgies and Sexation

Dear Applicant for Arrest

During our monthly search and sweep
We noticed your copy of How to Be a Sheep
Was missing from your apartment
And it is important
To develop a good citizen
We searched the cupboards and trash and recycling bin
But our search turned up nothing
Did you lose it or stolen by a criminal ring
You can replace the film 3 times
Before it become a crime
Our record says you've only lost one
However you did not notify us of the lost copy so you will be shunned
And we will not give you another copy
Because we are not very happy
Instead we will rearrest you
And under rearrest UA 000.32
You will have to watch How to Be a Sheep for 24 hours
Until you are a good and obedient citizen under our power
See you when you sleep
The Committee of Sheep

Dear Applicant for Arrest

Due to our new transient policy
You are being zoned out of our community
You will no longer able to stand on the sidewalk
Or panhandle or talk
Between the hours of 9 to 5 o'clock
Save money or keep food stocked
Since you are jobless and homeless
This will be your first and final notice
Under Disposing of the Homeless 003.542
We will terminate you
Incinerate your body
Sincerely the Bureau of Detritus Useless and Sorry

Dear Applicant for Arrest

We appreciate your application
And enjoyed all your criminal participation
But we cannot arrest you
For not enjoying wearing the color blue
At your casual Friday fiestas or
Not sharing your ideas when they were asked for
It is best for your boss to kill you
Under your contract clause 011.002
The employer can terminate the employee
When they do not express themselves freely
Thank you
Good luck with your boss kills you

Dear Applicant for Arrest

We have had complaints
That you will not write or paint
Due to your depression
Which seems to be prolonged by the recession
Under the Law of Creative Expression
You have to make art in order to feel passion
But instead you are refuse and do nothing
And the medication and Humiliation Therapy do not seem to be helping
Under Art Therapy AT 006.792
We will use forced inspiration and creatively torture you
We hope to leave an impression
Sincerely the Office of Creative Expression

Anxiété

that man made

that man made out great fishing today on that man made
lake near the factory where that man made nuts and bolts
for cars but that man made an explosion to get that man
made insurance figuring it was better than that man made it
out alive

down the road

down the road from here is my house go down pass the
traffic light and take a right down the roads drifting apart
one points east and the other goes up and dips down the
road is slippery watch out they're coming with salt from
down the road is out so take the bridge a little down the
road construction is loud and won't be finished until
Tuesday or maybe someday on down the road

on the job

on the job never off don’t stop smiling never on the job
training learning how to clean scrub wash your hands on
the job don’t relax always be looking for customers
wondering on the job never home going to and from work
maybe not on and on the job Friday closing and opening
upon the job interview for new employees wearing ties and
sitting on the job until Friday then sleeping on the job

what but the

what but the food is cold and no one wants to eat it now
what but the mood of the old people has been good lately
since we've instituted mandatory nap time what but the
what no then what but the world will go on without us what
but the girl still knows about us what but the fuck do you
mean

here to help

please sir stop yelling I'm only here to help bring out the
food for the customers it's almost time to open and stand
near the entrance over here to help with volunteering I love
working for the under privileged I give my time here to
help drive canned goods to the church for the here to help
written in bubble letters on t-shirts worn by an army of
people here to help bring together communities including
here to help pick up your brother from school where here to
help as gun shots ring out here to help build the fence
separating neighbors over there and here to help form an
orderly line for food you don't belong in this line but the
line over here to help wipe the blood off the police car here
to help us you'll need to smile here to help but work
without pay here to help pile the bodies here to help
disinfect the air here to help the smell of corpses here to
help but excuse me sir we're only here to help

everything but nickels

the new world is great we have everything freedom liberty all of that everything but nickels to pay for my coffee but I usually have enough to pay for everything but nickels are excepted in the soda machine dimes quarters bills even pennies everything but nickels now I have to make change and I hate having pennies well you can't have everything but nickels

but what was

but what was here first trees or rows of houses with but what was the point of arguing with him when he was drinking and not waiting but what was the town like when we moved I was just a baby I only remember but what was that honey I couldn't hear you over the news but what was he like before he died I can't but what was the question I only heard the answer but what was here won't but what was can't be again can’t you see

can’t you see the smoke rising from down the street no I
can’t you see there in that paragraph says the insurance
doesn’t cover fire so you can’t you see the fire on the news
two dead can’t you see I don’t have any money for food I
can’t you see I don’t love you anymore it’s over why can’t
you see you’re going to overload the circuit can’t you see
Joey I think he’s still inside all that smoke can’t you seen
the extra keys I can’t you see father can’t you see I’m
burning

the next war

and for the next war there will be fewer causalities I
promise because in the next war nothing but automation for
the next war women will be in the next war be more subtle
all that banging won't keep you up in the next war won't
cost a thing so the next war will be the last no more after
the next war but before we start the next war perhaps we
should finish the last

used to be

yeah well people don't treat me well but I'm used to be a
couch that broke from over used to be a coffee shop but
now it's a store that sells used to be people were polite
dressed nice and didn't used to be the world where it used
to be isn't what it used to be now that you're gone

trouble with doors

the trouble with doors they don’t shut the right trouble with
doors the locks don’t work and get in trouble with doors
voices carry trouble with doors muffle through the trouble
with doors loudly slam shut like trouble with doors always
listening to conversations about the trouble with doors off
the hinges and trouble with doors can’t afford not to listen
to trouble with doors silence without privacy

as if still

as if still a choice was made but as if still this course forces hope for things to change as if still nothing moves in the room as if still against the law to act as if still on the water the lake placid as if still escape the idea appeals as if still a solution as if still it still matters

it’s not that

it’s not that I hate you it’s not that shirt you wanted it’s not
that neighbor the other guy on the other side who thinks it’s
not that bad just a scratch no need to bring insurance into
it’s not that I don’t like you I don’t like that it’s not that
tree you ran into

not a member

she stands outside the store she is not a member of the
community laugh and celebrate not a member of this family
so pack your things you're not a member of the committee
voted to help homeless with housing saying it's not a
member of this coop anymore for not paying rent not a
member and now packing her life into boxes making a
shape of all the things she is not a membership fee missed
in 30 years and not a member of this store can afford to
miss a chance at this sale

an implied stop

not a rolling stop but an implied stop means fuck off as if
an implied stop at an intersection not a complete stop but
an implied stop yelling or you'll be kicked out it's not a
threat only an implied stop not to be taken seriously but
still the letter states an implied stop reaching for the
mashed potatoes ask for an implied stop to let the traffic go

I’m so sorry

I’m so sorry but we’re out of coffee can I get you something else like I’m so sorry about your father a good man I’m so sorry again but we’re about to close so I’m so sorry but we don’t take quarters so I’m so sorry I can’t help you with I’m so sorry you can’t sit there could you please leave I’m so sorry for your loss a bus stop

there's a bus stop fifteen minutes away from a bus stop
pissed off stranded waiting for a bus stop is dirty and sticky
when is there a bus stop touching a bus stop the bleeding
from my nose I could've walked a bus stop waiting to go
home

if you want

if you want to leave then leave no one is keeping you here if you want food there's food in the frig if you want we can go to the movies tomorrow but if you want to today they're having a sale on jeans if you want coffee order some but only if you want

all the lines

all the lines on the map divide and label countries
independent and segregate all the lines keep barbarians out
away from all the lines lead to Rome the center of all the
lines are clotting waiting to rupture into all the lines erase
all the lines but what did all the lines ever do to you